Journey to Freedom

POEMS, PRAYERS AND PROMISES

JON WOOD

Guardian
B O O K S

Belleville, Ontario, Canada

Journey to Freedom

Copyright © 2005, Jon Wood

Scripture quotations except those noted below are taken from the Holy Bible, Old and New Testaments, King James Version, Copyright© 1976 by Thomas Nelson, Inc. Used by permission of Thomas Nelson, Inc. All rights reserved.

Scripture quotations marked NIV are taken from the Holy Bible, New International Version®. Copyright© 1973,1978, 1984 by International Bible Society. Used by permission of Zondervan Publishing House. All rights reserved.

Library and Archives Canada Cataloguing in Publication

Wood, Jon (Jon R.)
      Journey to freedom : poems, prayers, and promises / Jon Wood.

ISBN 1-55306-862-9.--ISBN 1-55306-864-5 (LSI ed.)

      1. Promises--Religious aspects--Christianity. 2. Spiritual life--Christianity. 3. Wood, Jon (Jon R.) 4. Christian life. I. Title.

BV4501.3.W65 2004   248.4   C2004-906804-0

For more information, please contact:

Jon Wood
P.O. Box 1963
Kingston WA 98346

Guardian Books is an imprint of *Essence Publishing,* a Christian Book Publisher dedicated to furthering the work of Christ through the written word. For more information, contact:

20 Hanna Court, Belleville, Ontario, Canada K8P 5J2.
Phone: 1-800-238-6376 • Fax: (613) 962-3055.
E-mail: publishing@essencegroup.com
Internet: www.essencegroup.com

Poems, Prayers, and Promises

This book is presented to:

From:

Date:

Occasion:

Comments:

Dedication

I dedicate this book to my loving wife, Linda Mary, for her daily devotion to God, years of prayer and ministry to me, and to Paul and Betty for sharing their generous love of family. Paul and Betty were old friends who loved the Lord; I will always cherish our loving friendship, fellowship, and kindred spirit. This poem is for Miss Linda:

The Bicycle

With her new bicycle,
I PROMISED a bell.

A comfortable seat,
padded with gel.

To be there to catch her,
when she fell.

Ready to help her up,
before the bruises tell.

To ride the longer and smoother
rail-trails for a spell.

TABLE OF CONTENTS

ourney to Freedom is Jon Wood's journey of faith: a collection of his own experiences of God's work in his life and of promises from God's Word that have impacted him. This book chronicles Jon's journey toward Christian maturity, through promises he made and kept, and through God's faithfulness to him and his family.

Life is an exercise of surrendering to God's will, giving up selfish motives and desires for what He wants in our lives, and it is in that process that we mature as Christians. Promises are an important part of life— promises that are *made* as well as promises that are *received*—but a promise *kept* is an anchor to the soul, whether a promise of man or of God. God's promises are an assurance of His faithfulness, and a challenge to trust Him each day.

God has given this book to Jon, even though he had no idea when he began writing it what he and Linda would personally face. Her battle with cancer has taught them that each new day is a step in trusting the promises of God. In the same way, we don't know the twists and turns our lives will take, but we do know God's promises are true. He gives them to us for what we are going through, even the things we will face tomorrow that we could never imagine.

I believe, as you have chosen to read this book, that God has a promise He wants to speak to your heart in what you're going through now, what you've gone through in the past, or what you'll face tomorrow. My prayer is that you will read this book, as the Apostle Paul said to the Philippians,

> *"[B]eing confident of this, that He who began a good work in you will carry it on to completion until the day of Christ Jesus"* (Philippians 1:6, NIV).

— Phil Kreiling, Pastor
Overland Park First Assembly of God
Overland Park, Kansas

ACKNOWLEDGEMENTS

I would like to thank Editor Janet Crews for her skill, patience, and personal interest. But most of all I appreciate her faith, prayers, and fellowship on Linda's and my behalf. I also want to recognize John Quanrud for his thoughtful portrayal of the old man. The book cover is a color print of "The Old Man" painted by John Quanrud. Mr. Quanrud is a Northwest Artist and a Signature Member of the National Watercolor Society.

The black and white picture on the back of the book was taken at our home several years ago by a friend and photographer, Richard Chaffee. Thank you Rick.

While I was writing this book, several draft copies passed through several hands. I would like to thank the following friends, whose hands turned pages and who provided constructive criticism long before the draft copies showed much promise or held much interest:

Linda Wood, Susan McDonald, Jim Conkright, Linda Skaggs, Janice Pishny, D.D.S., Regina Thierry, Pastor Phil Kreiling, Marcia Christian, Trent Carter, Galen Wagner, Doug Strickland, Terry Maness, Theretha Worsham, Lisa Wright, Michele Lewis, Kenny Cohrs, Mila Reid, Roger and Katoo Sherrard, Tom and Kathy McAfee, Kathleen Brown, and Gloria Trivano.

To those who helped me write this book in other ways—by lending an ear, providing an encouraging word, or seeking God's blessing in prayer—I offer my sincere appreciation and gratitude.

And to Essence Publishing, I would like to give a special thanks to the Project Editor, Andrew Mackay, for his commitment to integrity, quality, and service.

This book features a painting of an old man, and it describes a remarkable story of inspiration, interpretation, and promise. The original watercolor painting, once called "The Old Man," is displayed in our home. Its message is both endearing and life-changing. In this book, I briefly describe my interpretation of the old man and how he inspired me.

The old man has a promise on which his eternal life depends. As I contemplated his promise, I developed a new sense of freedom in which more of myself was revealed. I was encouraged by the old man's transparency, so much so that I lowered my walls of protection, searched my heart and soul for God's purpose and direction, and responded to His truth by accepting the Lord as my salvation: *"And ye shall know the truth, and the truth shall make you free"* (John 8:32).

According to the artist, the painting of the old man is a composite; but for me, he was a prerequisite. Whether it was my perception of the old man that the artist intended to capture—pure serendipity—or the Holy Spirit's prompting is not what matters. What matters is that I have a committed relationship with Jesus Christ where, before my encounter with the old man, I did not.

What I see when I look at the old man is the promise he is making to God. As I began to study him and his promise, I gained a deeper appreciation for promises—especially God's promises. I started with the old man's promise to God, which led me to my promise to God and then to the promises that God has given to all mankind, but more specifically those He has given me.

God's promises are all-powerful—they can give us comfort and peace, sustain our needs, and be the answers to our prayers. This is the same power that works against our enemies and for our good, and if what's at work is the power of reciprocity, it is pressed down, shaken together, and overflowing:

> Give, and it shall be given unto you; good measure, pressed down, and shaken together, and running over, shall men give into your bosom. For with the same measure that ye mete withal it shall be measured to you again (Luke 6:38).

I set out to find God's truth. I searched my present and then my past, looking for evidence and proof that He was at work in my life. I started by contemplating my early adult years and the more I contemplated, the more I became aware and the more I became aware, the more I wanted to let go and let the love of Christ fill my mind, heart, and soul. This is when I realized how much I needed God and wanted His perfect love for my life.

God created the heavens and the earth. He is our cornerstone—He is the God we serve. His Word is our foundation and our strength, and it is in the name of Jesus Christ that He can move and work in our lives. When we read, listen, and pray with a heart for God, it is the Holy Spirit who delivers God's meaning; He is the one who brings us understanding and helps us to apply God's Word to our lives.

I wanted to fill the old man's life with my new-found appreciation and answered prayer. I imagined various types of promises for him—some were small and trivial, while others had the power of influence. I began this book by imagining the old man's promise, but I was soon examining my own.

By reaching back several years in my memory, I realized that some of my promises impacted my child-hood, some my teenage years, and some my adulthood. The promises vary, from driving a friend to the Seattle-Tacoma International Airport, to modeling pullover sweaters; from graduating from college, to accepting Jesus Christ as my Lord and Savior. They are endearing and life-changing promises—promises that I can recall or acknowledge. As this book describes each promise in its own way as a separate anecdote, it recognizes that promises—like people—come in all shapes and sizes.

Some promises have dominion, others bless and console, but the more we make God's business our business, the less we have to control. Being obedient to God gives Him a chance to work in our lives—to use our faithfulness for good and to bring about his purpose. It is by His love, mercy, and grace He makes us whole.

Chapter three, "Promises in Retrospect," is a review that encourages a promise-maker to be a promise-keeper. It goes beyond the universal definition for a promise by explaining how to create an *environment for keeping promises*: acknowledging that life has its own set of God-created promises, and using a metaphor to help demonstrate the ease of *making* a promise in contrast to *keeping* the same.

The "Prayers" in chapter eight are for the love of the Lord. They express love and devotion, praise and worship, while seeking God's presence and perfect will.

Most of the other chapters in this book have contributed both idea and word to the prose and poems found in chapter nine. Thus, the prose and poems express a second time, but in a different way, the importance of making and keeping promises.

God wants us to be faithful and obedient, and to share His love; what better way than through poems, prayers, and promises? My desire is that this book will glorify God by allowing Him to draw us closer, and that it will serve as a frequent reminder for those readers who are new in their faith.

Inspiration Taken From the Old Man

This chapter explains "what" inspired me to write this book, but given 20/20 hindsight, I can now look back and see "why" I wrote it.

I finished the majority of the book the same month that my wife Linda was diagnosed with pancreatic cancer. Since the diagnosis, we have experienced many blessings—in so many well orchestrated situations, in such a short period of time—that I am convinced we are in the shadow of His wings:

> *How excellent is thy lovingkindness, O God! therefore the children of men put their trust under the shadow of thy wings* (Psalm 36:7).

I feel writing this book was no coincidence. I believe God used this past year to prepare us for the road ahead. I pray that God's love, mercy, and grace shines over all those who know and love Him.

Call unto me, and I will answer thee, and show thee great and mighty things, which thou knowest not (Jeremiah 33:3).

CHAPTER ONE

Inspiration Taken From the Old Man

Occasionally, a person has an experience that strikes a true chord, and that chord continues to resonate until it has permeated his or her entire being. That is what happened to me three years ago in a frame and fine art gallery in downtown Poulsbo, Washington.

Poulsbo is a small Norwegian town that borders Liberty Bay. West, across the bay, are the Olympic Mountains, and together, the mountains and the bay create a majestic and picturesque setting. I was browsing in Deb's Frame Gallery when I first saw the painting of the old man. It was on the floor, leaning against the wall in an alcove. After what seemed to be only seconds, I knew that the old man and I shared a common bond—an affinity. In retrospect, I would say he and I share a thread of independence, desire, and broken promises.

The artist, John Quanrud, painted the old man in 1988. Although I bought the painting the same day I first saw it, I didn't see it until June of 2000. It took twelve years before the artist was willing to let the painting go, but fortunately, I was in the right place at the right time. The gallery was putting on an exhibit featuring the Northwest artist's paintings and the composite of the old man was among his works. When I asked the gallery's owner (Debbie) for the painting's name and about its title, she said it was called "The Old Man," and that either of us could contact the artist about the title.

After I acquired the painting, I contacted the artist to find out if he had given the painting a title. Mr. Quanrud said it was untitled, and then kindly asked if I had a title in mind. I wanted a title with stature equivalent to the strength of the painting itself. Calling it "The Old Man" was a way to identify it from all the other paintings, but I felt it would ultimately need a distinct title of its own. After considering several names, I selected "I Promise" as the title that I thought best captured the painting, feeling it appropriately introduced both the painting and its subject.

The painting captivated me from the start. I wanted to know the old man, to interpret his story, and then to share my interpretation with others. After two years, I decided to step out in faith to see if writing this book was part of God's plan for me. Inspired by the old man and his promise, I was eager to write about promises—past and present.

The watercolor painting was the initial inspiration for this book, but gradually the old man's promise became my primary motivation. The painting is of an older man who, by his appearance and expression, is communicating from deep within his soul. He is looking outward, and his eyes are telling a story. His demeanor is decisive—yet, at the same time, it displays an aspect of peace that is absolute.

I never imagined that the old man would become my psuedo form of accountability. Those of us who desire more spiritual accountability will often ask another believer to be our confidant, someone to whom we will be accountable; but for me, seeing the old man every day for two years was my reminder, form of reference, accountability, and proof. Biblical prophecy tells us, *"[Y]our old men will dream dreams and your younger men will see visions"* (Joel 2:28). In like manner, I believe it was the Holy Spirit who prompted me to be accountable to the Lord.

I accepted Christ as my Savior in 1983 before moving from California to Washington, but I still had not surrendered to Christ as Lord of my life. For the next seventeen years, I kept control of my life, acknowledging Jesus, but not allowing Him to be my

Lord. My old nature remained sovereign, a free spirit unchecked, unaccountable, and dissatisfied.

Then, in August of 2000, a job transfer took my wife Linda and me from Washington to the Midwest. As we prepared to move, the painting of the old man was wrapped and sealed, where it remained undisturbed until we were established in our new home. Once Linda and I were settled, we selected a prominent place to hang the painting. From the moment the old man was put on display, it seemed as though he had something I wanted, even before I knew what it was or how to get it.

He seemed to be in the presence of God. The more I eyed him, the more I thought about to whom he was praying, and what his prayer might be. I began to see the promise he was making to God—to die to self and to live a life for Christ.

Without realizing it, my desire to study the old man and his circumstances was profound; I had no idea what would transpire when I acknowledged the old man and his commitment to God. I didn't know that it would move me to do the same, and led me to commit my own life to God.

Finally, the day came when I began to see Jesus as my Lord and Savior. I could feel a peace building within me, filling my heart with praise. I felt God replacing my darkness with light, my sadness with joy—I could feel Him lifting my troubles and pain. I believe the Holy

Spirit was encouraging me to give my life to God, to trust and obey Him, and to lay my burdens at His feet.

It took the old man, his promise, and many answered prayers before I finally surrendered. For a moment my life stood still, and in that instant, I felt free to follow Jesus— to submit myself unto the Lord—to desire His will rather than my own, and to ask Him to be the Lord of my life.

The Lord has promised that, *"Being confident of this very thing, that he which hath begun a good work in you will perform it until the day of Jesus Christ"* (Philippians 1:6). I like what this promise gives me—blessed assurance that everything is in His hands and in His time.

The Interpretation of the Old Man

This chapter presents a candid view of an old man's journey to freedom. The old man knows Jesus as Lord and Savior, and because he does, he has a newborn freedom that comes only from knowing Christ: *"Jesus saith unto him, I am the way, the truth, and the life: no man cometh unto the Father, but by me"* (John 14:6).

For the old man, each day is a blessing and prayerfully a good day, as for tomorrow, it is a blessed time for renewing the promise he made today.

> *Therefore if any man be in Christ, he is a new creature: old things are passed away; behold, all things are become new* (2 Corinthians 5:17).

CHAPTER TWO

The Interpretation of the Old Man

The original painting of the old man is an object of art appreciation, and it provides the theme for this book. After thoughtful examination, I surmised that the subject and theme underlying the old man and his promise share a fundamental question: "What gives a promise, promise?"

God's word is the foundation and underpinning of strength, courage, and power that our promises rely on to confront and conquer our old carnal natures. our commitment to "seek first His kingdom and to surrender to His will," is what gives a promise, promise. For example: we are to ask the Holy Spirit for His wisdom whenever wisdom is needed, and to praise God whenever we believe that something was His provision and not ours.

I feel the more we live our faith, the more we'll choose His wisdom over our own, and in doing so, we will inevitably be honoring Him. He is the Alpha and the Omega—the beginning and the end.

In my opinion the question, "What gives a promise, promise?" is crucial. It's answer is key to keeping the spirit of a promise alive. Hopefully, the answers provided in this book will become a means of support and encouragement to anyone who intends to honor God and himself by keeping his word. God uses our faithfulness to both strengthen and bind relationships, thereby glorifying Himself and blessing the faithful.

My interpretation of the painting starts out with the old man standing on familiar ground, making the same promise to die to self and to live for Christ—only this time, he is making it at God's altar. I felt compelled to write about how it would be for the old man to seek, and then to relinquish himself unto the Lord. His attention has turned toward eternal life, where his soul will abide in God's love, glory, and grace. When I examined my interest surrounding the old man, there was but one explanation that stood above all the rest—the Lord was using the fact that we lived far from home and family to bring my wife and me closer to Him, and to each other.

I could see the connection—the old man was making a sincere promise in a private moment between his Maker and himself. He was focused, committed, devoted, and willing to accept any consequence. When I focused on the old man, I saw a father figure: a man with responsibilities, obligations, and compassion. I saw a man who would ask for healing for his child and forgiveness for himself, or question, "Lord, why me?"

Despite its being two-dimensional, I never tire studying the painting of the old man or wanting to confirm my impression of him. I feel he is my responsibility. I have checked on him nearly every day for the past two years. I have given the old man more than a casual glance—I have examined him in detail, close enough to see that he is intent and filled with a genuine anticipation for God.

When I look at the old man, I see what is tangible—something with which I can identify. His face is the face of a man who has led an honest life, not without hardships, but one that he is thankful for and has judged to be good. In most cases, "good" was a life that rolled along until some disaster, natural or unnatural, occurred. Oddly enough, it is in times of disaster that we turn to God. Disasters will change your perspective in a heartbeat, causing your knees to find a comfortable kneeling position from which to pray.

The old man never liked being told that "Our eyes are the windows to our soul." He felt indignant about what was required. He wanted to "live and let live"—to turn away and deny the fact of his body as a temple of the Holy Spirit. Instead, he underestimated the importance of protecting his soul from what the eyes can see.

While the old man remembers paying for his wisdom at the expense of his innocence, he is no longer the same man he once was. He has changed, and today, his confidence is where it belongs: in Christ the Lord. I see him seeking wisdom from the Lord, blessed by a deep desire for more knowledge, understanding, and insight.

This has brought me to these questions: "What is wisdom? How do you obtain it? For what purpose, and to what end?" I wanted to grasp the importance of wisdom, so I began searching for the answers to these questions.

I found answers in 1 Kings. According to the Bible, King David named Solomon to be the new king. Then, in a dream, God said to Solomon, "*Ask what I shall give thee*" (1 Kings 3:5). Solomon asked for wisdom, not for the lives of his enemies or riches for himself. Because of this, God said, "*Behold, I have done according to thy words*" (1 Kings 3:12).

God is able to meet our daily needs in the same way He met Solomon's:

God gave Solomon wisdom and very great insight, and a breadth of understanding as measureless as the sand on the seashore. Solomon's wisdom was greater than the wisdom of all the men of the East, and greater than all the wisdom of Egypt. He was wiser than any other man, including Ethan the

Ezrahite-wiser than Heman, Calcol and Darda, the sons of Mahol. And his fame spread to all the surrounding nations (1 Kings 4:29–31, NIV).

We are to ask the Lord for wisdom as Solomon did. *"Counsel is mine, and sound wisdom: I am understanding; I have strength"* (Proverbs 8:14).

The old man was trusting in himself, relying solely on his own daily observations and experiences. He was comfortable assuming that wisdom was one of life's residual benefits, but his life began to change after he learned what the Bible—specifically Proverbs 1 and 2—had to say on the subject. Proverbs 1:7 states that *"The fear of the LORD is the beginning of knowledge."* Proverbs 2:6 adds *"out of his mouth cometh knowledge and understanding."* The old man wanted to know the truth.

Recently, our pastor spoke of having a good life without Christ. He said that he believed it was possible. Hearing this in church, from our senior pastor, was puzzling—until he finished by saying, "But are you willing and ready to *die* without Christ?"

To paraphrase, what I heard him say was that a person may choose to live without Christ, but would never want to die without Him. Those who die without Christ, die without salvation, and are isolated and separated from God for eternity. I believe the old man came to the same conclusion before he decided to reject his old inner nature and surrender his life unconditionally to Christ.

The old man was taught to say, "You do your part, and I'll do mine." He meant well, and in good faith, this is what he had said, but he doesn't want to say it anymore. Now he sees how his advice was conditional, and his commitments were contingent upon the unforeseen.

Today, he knows that he lives by grace, and that his desire to listen and be obedient to God is righteous. From now on, he will develop an attitude of living for Christ and will stop his self-destructive ways.

I see the old man saying, "Lord, I surrender all." He had been a man who, between crises, thought he was in control, and until now was never quite ready to surrender to God's will. Yet, somehow, he knows it is time to obey—it is time for him to say, "I promise Lord, this time is different—this time I will abide in You."

> *Therefore if any man be in Christ, he is a new creature: old things are passed away; behold, all things are become new* (2 Corinthians 5:17).

Recently, I was listening to a pastor on the radio and I immediately fell for what he said: "God helps the people who help themselves." Then he reversed course and said, "It may sound biblical, but this saying is not in the Bible." According to the pastor, the Bible tells us that God helps those who *cannot* help themselves:

> *For he shall deliver the needy when he crieth; the poor also, and him that hath no helper. He shall*

spare the poor and needy, and shall save the souls of the needy (Psalm 72:12–13).

He continued by explaining that for those who are content, God will bless others through their contentment. He will use their abundance for good, and bless them in return. God can do this because He is an almighty God with a good plan. He is omnipresent, omniscient, and omnipotent—meaning He is all-present, all-knowing, and all-powerful.

It is awesome to discover that God has a plan and a purpose for each of us; to know that He is in charge, that we are connected to God through our faith in Christ; and that He is ready to open His arms to us even if we have previously rejected Him:

Behold, I stand at the door, and knock: if any man hear my voice, and open the door, I will come in to him, and will sup with him, and he with me (Revelation 3:20).

Promises in Retrospect

We begin learning about promises early in our lives. Some of our first lessons, in fact, are the result of being on the learning end of a promise. It doesn't matter which end you are on: you can learn from making a promise, receiving a promise, or both.

I believe promises are partially defined by the same set of common truths they share. Some of the less-evident common truths are the premise for this chapter.

Give, and it shall be given unto you; good measure, pressed down, and shaken together, and running over, shall men give into your bosom. For with the same measure that ye mete withal it shall be measured to you again (Luke 6:38).

CHAPTER THREE

Promises in Retrospect

B y definition, a promise is: "a pledge, claim or declaration by one or more individuals, to one or more individuals, to either do something specified or to show restraint by doing nothing." To be more precise, a promise is "either a performance or a forbearance of a specified act" (*Webster's Ninth New Collegiate Dictionary*, 1988, Merriam-Webster Inc., Springfield, Massachusetts).

Whether or not a promise requires performance, its hopes and expectations remain constant. Promises embrace free choice and endure time while waiting for fruition. They are self-acknowledged commitments we make to God, ourselves, and to other people.

Promises can start out as one type of commitment and end up as another. Some have the power to change lives while others merely endear. Although there are several kinds of promises—including allegiances, oaths, pledges, and vows—this book only focuses on two: endearing and life-changing. Those that endear give us ways to instantly satisfy and bless one another, while life-changing promises may require that we wait for tangible results before we can assess how or to what extent our lives have been changed.

God will take our steps of faith, no matter how small, and put them into motion—thus causing a chain reaction that will change our lives as we strive to accomplish His perfect will. Being obedient to God changes lives; it gives Him a chance to work in our lives to bring about His purpose. For example, when two people are engaged, they have promised themselves to each other. In short, they are engaged to be married, and it is this mutual promise of love that is perfected through their mutual love for Jesus Christ.

The Bible is God's truth, wisdom, and living Word, and it is this book's foundation. When we combine *this* foundation with our faithfulness, obedience, and tangible and intangible resources, we create an *environment for keeping promises*. The combinations of resources are endless. The tangibles and intangibles could range from time, money, and material to forgiveness, patience, and prayer, respectively.

Given that the combinations of tangibles and intangibles for a promise are infinite, this book does not try to define them. Instead, it asks the reader to fill in the spaces, assuming that each combination is a promise in the making.

Most people have reasons for doing things, and making promises is no exception. A reason may be fundamental and come from Scripture, or superficial and come from everyday life. Despite its origin, the reason must make sense, be reasonable, show cause, or have more than an element of truth. For as long as the reason is unworthy, the promise will be, too.

The truth of fulfilling a promise remains. When a promise is consummated, it can bolster, console, and encourage. It sets a good precedent, and has the capacity to increase and maintain credibility, integrity, and reverence. Keeping a promise may also mitigate otherwise serious consequences, strengthen the respect you have for yourself and others, and as a natural progression, will advance in concert with life's promises.

Life has its own set of promises created by God for all mankind. They are passed from generation to generation without exception. Some of these promises we accept gracefully and attribute to human nature; others we learn the hard way and credit natural law. Either way, the lessons we learn from life's promises are ours to keep; they become part of our living legacies to old age.

Consequences are a signficant part of life's promises, especially when we wait for the Holy Spirit, life, or life's circumstances to remind us that we have promises to keep. When we break one too many promises, we break the bank, in a manner of speaking. And in an instant we can find out that breaking the bank has had a negative effect on those whom we love the most.

The person who fails to keep his promises may find the consequences are long-lasting and nearly impossible to reverse. This fact alone merits our respect and is reason enough for a person to strive to keep his or her promises, lest we forget *why* we strive to keep our promises in the first place!

God wants to bless all of our promises. To Him, *a promise is a promise*, and its size and importance are irrelevant. Whether *a promise is a promise* is considered a moral truism or not, promises will have their own unique set of circumstances that are seldom equivalent.

I believe when we keep our promises the Holy Spirit uses our faithfulness for good. This way, when the results of a promise exceed our expectations or surpass our wildest dreams, we have the Holy Spirit to thank. I see "This way" as God's provision, and this deed as yet another reason for us to keep our promises.

In the final analysis, when a person fulfills a promise in faith, fellowship, and obedience God's love is manifested, nurtured and preserved. This manifestation is revealed as fruit of the Spirit, it's God's love that we make visible through our love, joy, peace, patience, kindness, goodness, faithfulness, gentleness, and self-control. It is a blessing for all concerned; then as the promise keeper gives praise to the Lord, he or she can redeem God's love and reclaim the fruit of the Spirit through Him. Returning God's love is a privilege. As we return His love, we are free to receive God's love anew, because God's love is then free to warm the soul and give peace of mind. The statement, "It is easier to make a promise than it is to keep one" has truth; but to hear someone say it is a reminder that every promise carries an underlying commitment. This commitment is what reflects our obedience and faithfulness to Christ.

If I were asked to write a metaphor illustrating the ease of making a promise, in contrast to keeping the same, my metaphor would read: if a finished promise could be a finished painting,

(1) the paint would be the pool of resources;

(2) the canvas would be the foundation of God; and,

(3) the frame would be the fear of the Lord.[1]

The truth is that most artists will start more paintings than they will finish, and buy more paint than they will use. In the same way, it is easier to make a promise than it is to keep one.

Scriptures remind us that, "*It is more blessed to give than to receive*" (Acts 20:35); and that "*God loveth a cheerful giver"* (2 Corinthians 9:7). When we make a promise, we give our word; and if someone is better off because of it, then keeping the promise is a blessing.

Notes

[1] *"The fear of the Lord is the beginning of knowledge:"* (Proverbs 1:7).

Endearing Promises

This chapter contains a few short stories to encourage the reader to remain thankful for past promises, to be a trigger for past memories, and to give the reader a reason to recall some of his or her own endearing or life-changing promises.

A promise that endears one to another, or edifies one or the other, can become a wonderful treasure to be cherished for a lifetime. *"For ye are all the children of God by faith in Christ Jesus"* (Galatians 3:26).

CHAPTER FOUR

Endearing Promises

Modeling Sweaters

One Christmas, I promised to take my wife Linda and one of our daughters shopping at the Seattle-Tacoma, South Center Mall. It was after Christmas, and we were bargain hunting.

All three of us went into a men's and women's clothing store, and before long, Linda was eyeing men's sweaters. Although she has trouble buying for herself, she easily buys for me. Naturally, I would have to try on the clothing for size and fit. Whenever we shop, we treat shopping as a joint endeavor, she shops for me, and I model for her.

On occasion I will buy clothing for Linda, but with the caveat that I keep it understated, elegant, and buy what's on sale.

I was across the aisle from Linda when she said, "Here is a large; see if it fits." She handed me the sweater, and I obliged her by taking off my coat. I pulled the sweater over my head and shoulders, but at that point I was stuck! The sweater and I became one: I could neither pull the sweater the rest of the way on, nor could I could pull it off. I think Linda started laughing first, and then all three of us began to laugh. The sweater turned out to be a "woman's large."

Although we considered the promise to go shopping a minor one, the memory continues to be a major blessing. I continue to be amazed at how, over time, God can take a small commitment and turn it into a huge blessing. When we are faithful to thank God for His love and blessings, our blessings become our joy all over again.

When we laugh at ourselves, I like to think the Holy Spirit smiles back.

The White Dove

I once promised to give a friend a ride to the airport. I wish I had asked God to reveal His love—it would have been so appropriate.

My friend Dale, who lives in Washington, has an ongoing music ministry. His friend Kevin was on a mission when he came to Washington to visit Dale. He only had a few days to visit, and then he would need a ride back to the airport. Dale had to work the day his friend was leaving, so I volunteered to drive Kevin to the airport.

As a youth, Kevin had been a pop musician, writing, singing and producing music. Music had been his ministry. However, in a few days, Kevin would be headed north to a church in Ketchikan, Alaska. He was going there to minister, only this time, he was going as *the* minister of the Clover Pass Community Church.

I was glad we had gone to our evening worship to see Kevin perform. Although Kevin and I had just met, I had the feeling that one door in his life was closing, while another door in his life was braced wide open. I knew Kevin was British before hearing him sing, but more important that his English accent, was his worship and praise for our King.

On the morning he was to depart, Kevin and I were on our way to the airport. I was driving a white Cadillac, going north on Interstate 5, heading toward the Seattle-Tacoma International Airport. I was doing about sixty-five miles per hour when a white dove came flying alongside my window. It stayed there for a while, passed us, and then flew straight ahead of the car. It remained ahead of the car long enough for each of us to say to the other, "What is going on?" Kevin was on his way to pastor a Christian Missionary Alliance church, and it looked like we had an escort.

It was remarkable! Eventually, the dove slowed until it was flying above us, and then it was gone. Afterwards, I glanced at the cars around us, looking for someone to confirm the dove; but no one did. Everyone was too busy driving. I have no idea why the dove appeared, but I do have a memory of our wondering if the dove was a message, a sign, or a promise from God.

Driving back from the airport, I thought again about the dove: was it riding an up-draft off the side of my car? I may never know for sure, but in my heart, I believe Kevin was in step with the Holy Spirit—and what we were seeing was God's perfect love.

In Los Angeles

During my grade school through high school years, we lived along the California coast, approximately seventy-five miles north of the Los Angeles basin.

My father's first visit to Minnesota was a precursor to other trips to Minnesota, all of which reflected his deep desire to see his home state again, and to be back on the farm. Although it's been several years since we moved west, it is still true and as our Kansas friend David Linehan would say, "You can take the boy out of the farm, but you can't take the farm out of the boy."

The following endearing memory began as an impulsive decision that started when my stepmother—intentionally or unconsciously—provided me with an excuse to miss a day of high school. My father had been halfway across country and was expected home later that day. My stepmother said that he would be arriving in Los

Angeles, California, by bus, but she did not know how he was going to get the rest of the way home. I assumed that *bus* meant a Greyhound bus. This opportunity was too irresistible for a lonely sixteen-year-old boy.

By my calculations, I had sufficient time to drive to Los Angeles and be there in time to pick up my dad. It seemed simple enough: all I had to do was drive my car, find Los Angeles, the Greyhound bus depot, the terminal, and my dad. That morning I promised myself that I would go get my dad. At sixteen, it seemed appropriate—at that age, timing has a lot to do with what is and what isn't appropriate.

I drove to Los Angeles, found the bus depot, and then went inside. I was running a little late, so I headed straight for the corridor marked "Arrivals." In the corridor, the light was dim and the floor was slightly inclined in the direction I was walking. My dad and I were both hurrying to get to our destinations, but we were walking in a straight line toward each other and didn't know it. When we met, we were both surprised. I had not thought about what to say, and he had no idea that I would be there to meet him. His initial reaction was to ask me, "What are you doing here?" Once I was able to speak, I blurted out, "I came to pick you up." A couple of minutes passed before I could relax and regain my composure—I had not expected to find him quite so soon.

The fact that I found the bus station and then was

able to find my dad was highly improbable. In part, that is why this memory is so special. The other part is, I like thinking that over time our greatest memories will become our greatest possessions. In any event, I will always be grateful for my promise, and that everything came together so perfectly.

Lucky the Hen

Lucky is a hen. When I think about how Lucky got her name, I am reminded of an endearing promise I made to one of our neighbors a few years back. Our neighbors were planning a fishing trip to eastern Washington. They would be gone a week or more, and needed someone to feed their chickens. When I promised to feed them, I didn't see any problems. The idea of losing control never crossed my mind.

For the first few days, everything went normally—I fed and watered the chickens, and gathered the eggs. Then disaster struck—the worst thing I could have imagined happened. The chicken coop was old and in disrepair, and I started finding feathers strewn around outside of it. So, I plugged the holes and made sure the fence was nailed securely around its frame. For the next few days, I experienced *déjà vu*. What little I could do to save the chickens was not enough: every day I would find more chicken feathers scattered outside the coop and one less chicken inside.

I began to worry that the rest of the chickens would be gone by the time my neighbors came home. From that day forward, I started marking off the remaining days, hoping there would be chickens left when my responsibility ended.

Our neighbors returned in time to find Lucky clinging to the rafters. She was the last chicken out of the dozen or more they had entrusted to me. I felt guilty about their loss, but after our neighbors bought more chickens and revamped the chicken coop, my guilt faded.

The last time I visited Lucky, there was a horseshoe nailed over her door, and she had lost her cluck. I wonder if she lost her cluck telling too many war stories to the new chicks!

Although my neighbors and I never found out what was killing the chickens, God has continued to bless our joint friendship. As friends, we continue making promises back and forth. Whenever either of us shares our faith through prayer, or stops to give thanks for what we have accomplished by the grace of God, our mutual friendship is strengthened and blessed.

Life-Changing Promises

This chapter contains life stories that describe life-changing promises. Some life-changing promises are planned commitments that we knowingly make for life, while others start out as everyday promises and then turn into life-changing promises somewhere along the way. Therefore, it is equally important to pray for both life-changing and endearing promises alike.

Our best reminder is to keep our eyes, ears, and hearts centered on Him:

I am the vine, ye are the branches: He that abideth in me, and I in him, the same bringeth forth much fruit: for without me ye can do nothing (John 15:5).

CHAPTER FIVE

Life-Changing Promises

Gaining Insight

B efore I learned to trim a sail or wax a pair of snow skis, I wanted to play football. It was the summer after my sophomore year in high school, and I was trying out for the varsity football team. I was intent on learning how to tackle, block, and memorize plays.

I didn't know it at the time, but my football career was about to end. Just before our first scheduled scrimmage game, my father came home with a 1957 Chevy and wanted me to quit football. He explained that we had a distant relative who had been seriously injured playing football, and he didn't want the same thing happening to me. My father said that if I would give up football and promise to earn enough money to pay for gas and car insurance, the car could be mine.

My father's concern was a judgement call, but I didn't care. I wanted the '57 Chevy. However, now when I look back, I can see another side: I see the chance I missed to represent my high school, play on a varsity football team, and do something that builds character, confidence, memories, and self-esteem.

For the next several years, I held my father responsible for not teaching me the values of discipline and the benefits of delayed gratification. Eventually, however, I came full circle. I began to realize that the choice had been mine, and that my father was right—at least about preserving one's own physical integrity.

Perhaps a part of me will always wish I had played football, but it's not always what you know or what you've done that's important. It is important *who* you know, notably Jesus Christ. He is our Lord and Savior, our salvation, our strength, and His truth will set us free.

I believe my natural father believed in God and knew Jesus as his Savior, but like me, he thought he had all the time in the world to ask Jesus to be his Lord. A person can have salvation without spiritual freedom, although spiritual freedom is the type of relationship God meant for us. Each time we call on God, and trust and lean on Him, we experience spiritual freedom. But it is not until we begin to choose Jesus as our Lord and Savior—day by day, hour by hour, minute by minute, and immersing ourselves in His love, mercy, and grace—that we become spiritually free.

And yet, spiritual freedom is more than a relationship, it is a defense against Satan. When a person has divided loyalties, he or she is spiritually weak and susceptible to attack. Have no doubt: our fight is spiritual, and Satan is the hungry lion. He is the deceiver. He will lie, cheat, and steal. He is not our friend, but our enemy. He seeks to kill, destroy, and to steal our very soul.

I believe spiritual freedom is on the right-side of right, and that it is our refuge against what is wrong. To the mature believer, having an honest and open relationship with our Lord and Savior Jesus Christ is a daily blessing and a Godsend.

As a young man, I didn't have the maturity to ask my father for his testimony, but I wish that I had. Today, as a father and grandfather, my prayer is for our entire family. I pray that each member will have their own testimony, understand its importance, and will want to share it with each other. Meanwhile, I'm thankful I had a father who cared.

The Day We Accepted Jesus

Accepting Jesus Christ as my Lord and Savior was a life-changing promise, but I lacked the catalyst that allows the Holy Spirit to take full control. In 1983, my wife and I did not attend church. As children we had both gone to church and Sunday school with our families, but in 1983 we were no longer church members. I thought I was too busy to attend church; in reality, I was too busy avoiding God.

We were living in Ventura, California, when we met a Soundman from the TV show "Hill Street Blues." He and his family lived about thirty miles south, near Highway 101 in Woodland Hills. A few weeks after meeting him, we were invited to his home. We accepted, and it turned out to be our one and only visit before we moved to Washington.

When we arrived, we had the pleasure of meeting his wife and young children. After introducing us to his family, he told us about his work, the Emmy Award for his "sound mixing" on "Hill Street Blues," and about his first love, Jesus Christ.

> In whom ye also trusted, after that ye heard the word of truth, the gospel of your salvation: in whom also after that ye believed, ye were sealed with that holy Spirit of promise (Ephesians 1:13).

That day in 1983, Linda and I both accepted Jesus Christ as our Lord and Savior. I remember thinking that now I was a new man—"born again"—and it was out with the old and in with the new. When a person invites Jesus Christ to be his Lord and Savior, he receives God's salvation. However, if he wants spiritual freedom by having Jesus Christ as his Lord and Master, he must first "die to self." Otherwise the will and desire in his life will be his own and not God's.

For God so loved the world, that he gave his only begotten Son, that whosoever believeth in him should not perish, but have everlasting life (John 3:16).

Although my old nature was the master, it was never satisfied and always wanted more. The choice is ours: either we cast out our old natures and seek the presence of our living God, or we will end up trying to serve two masters:

No man can serve two masters: for either he will hate the one, and love the other; or else he will hold to the one, and despise the other. Ye cannot serve God and mammon (Matthew 6:24).

For twenty years I tried to prove Matthew 6:24 wrong; either I loved myself and hated God, or I held to myself and despised God. At the very least, I was spiritually stuck "surrendering to Jesus as my Lord," and at the very best, my old nature had overstayed its welcome.

For some people, it happens all at once—the old nature dies, and the Holy Spirit moves in. However, when the Holy Spirit moved into my life, my old nature became an expatriate who maintained the status quo until I encountered the old man's painting seventeen years later. I would have never imagined that seeing the old man "dying to self" and relinquishing control to God would have moved me to do the same.

After watching the old man for two years, I finally realized that if I wanted Jesus Christ to be my Lord and Master, I first had to set my will aside and make room for his, *"For ye are all the children of God by faith in Christ Jesus"* (Galatians 3:26). Like the old man discovered, "Each day is a blessing and prayerfully a good day, as for tomorrow, it is a blessed time for renewing the promise he made today." Thank You, Lord!

Although experience is a good teacher and we all may become God's children, we never have the same *exact* experience of Him. When people talk about their walks with the Lord, or about having a personal relationship with God, no two accounts are ever the same.

> *Therefore if any man be in Christ, he is a new creature: old things are passed away; behold, all things are become new* (2 Corinthians 5:17).

Graduating From College

It took most of my adult life to realize one of my dreams and to fulfill one of my promises—graduating from college. One of my motivators was our children. I thought that our children, those still without a degree, might notice, be encouraged or follow suit. As of this writing, two of our four children are attending college.

One daughter is pursuing her master's degree, while our youngest son is in junior college.

As if foreordained, my obtaining a degree inspired my wife Linda. Although she was working, she returned to college to pursue certification as a paralegal. This taught me that when we keep a promise, we have no idea how far it will go or who it will reach.

I am encouraged by the thought of God using our completed promises or faithful endeavors to further His Kingdom. Linda's efforts, at the very least, generated a noticeable degree of shared respect and self-satisfaction.

In May of 2000, the Pacific Northwest was our home. I had just completed an undergraduate program and was looking for a new job. I wanted to combine my education with my experience and let "destiny" be our guide. At the time, we were prepared to move if the right job came along. Our one concern was Linda's job, but we agreed to cross that bridge when we came to it.

Once I finished college, I wanted to use my education. I was hoping for a better job near home, but at the same time, I was willing to go where the work was. By summer's end, I had been offered a job with the Department of Agriculture in Kansas City, Missouri. It was an opportunity for me to use my training, education, and update my skills—all in one place at one time.

Shortly after I had accepted the offer, Linda and I changed jobs, churches, and everything in between.

Fortunately, we found a wonderful church in Overland Park, Kansas. Over time it became one of our greatest blessings. It was there we learned a vital lesson: the more we are in His presence, the more He will change us—and the more we will know His perfection.

Looking back at my time in college, I can see a pair of dynamics at work. The first was obtaining the degree, and the second was the journey itself. I can apply a simple question to my experience: "Which is more important, the destination or the journey?" In this comparison, a college degree is the destination, and the journey is what it takes to earn the degree. Although the answers are subjective, experience reveals that achieving a college degree provides the graduate with a fundamental boost, and what the person gains along the way in terms of understanding, capability, and wisdom is his or hers to develop, use, and build on.

My experience tells me education may be more about having a future than a fortune: *"But my God shall supply all your need according to his riches in glory by Christ Jesus"* (Philippians 4:19).

Twenty-Three Years of Marriage

When two people celebrate twenty-three years of marriage together, like Linda and I have, we see that marriage was and is a life-changing promise. It reminds me of a Sunday morning sermon when our pastor told us salvation is both an event and a process. He told us, "Once you are saved, you still have to work out your salvation."

Marriage is like that—after your wedding, you still have to work out your marriage. It is a process, but when marriage is held in honor before God, it has the power of the love of Jesus Christ.

After twenty-three years of marriage, it is still a process, but when it's under God's control, He will perfect it and turn it into a lifelong process as well. It's God's desire to work in our lives and by working in our lives, He works in our marriages. His Word tells us that marriage is good,[1] and to rejoice in what is good.[2] As a married believer, I pray "our marriage is a blessing and it glorifies God."

Before I "died to self" and surrendered to Christ, I was resisting the Lord. When I was at church, I would read and sing along to most of the words on the visual overhead, but occasionally I would skip a verse. When I came to words like, "I live for God alone," I would have to skip them and go to the next verse.

In good faith I could not sing the verse, "I live for God alone," because I was not living for God alone. I took this phrase literally, and when I did, the words seemed unbelievable, unreasonable, and unrealistic. I even questioned my being a Christian. In retrospect, I was resisting the Holy Spirit and not submitting to God's truth.

Today, I get a different message when I read "I live for God alone." Now, I understand it is not a one-time, black-and-white event—rather, it is a daily choice one makes. It is saying, "God, use me, and let Your will be done in me and through me." As our associate pastor said, "We are to practice being in the presence of our Living God; in His presence, I am changed." His is real—He is present, and He lives:

> Ye have not chosen me, but I have chosen you, and ordained you, that ye should go and bring forth fruit, and that your fruit should remain: that whatsoever ye shall ask of the Father in my name, he may give it you (John 15:16).

Notes

[1] *"Whoso findeth a wife findeth a good thing"* (Proverbs 18:22).

[2] *"[L]et thy saints rejoice in goodness"* (2 Chronicles 6:41).

Standing on the Promises of God

This chapter contains anecdotes to affirm God's presence and love. These are different personal accounts of how prayers, through faith, were answered. Sometimes we look back and wonder how we survived childhood. However, when Christ is our Savior, we have reason to know.

I hope that, throughout these stories, you will see God at work and be reminded to pray—not only for your immediate family, but for the proverbial child next door. When I look back at my accounts, I am left knowing our need for God is real.

And he said unto me, My grace is sufficient for thee: for my strength is made perfect in weakness. Most gladly therefore will I rather glory in my infirmities, that the power of Christ may rest upon me (2 Corinthians 12:9).

CHAPTER SIX

Standing on the Promises of God

Swimming in the Ocean

The Scriptures tell us our faith can move mountains, and that our prayers connect us with God. I believe this is God's will and His providence for us. Thus, these truths are ours to claim.

When you grow up along the California coast, going the beach is a frequent ritual. Every summer, kids from the local area either walk or ride their bikes to the beach. I have many memories of those times at the beach, both bad and good. I remember strong rip tides that could pull you out to sea, and nights when you could see the phosphorous in the waves as they were breaking on the beach. Sometimes, swimming after dark, we could see the phosphorous on our bodies glowing like neon lights. *"Call unto me, and I will answer thee, and show thee great and mighty things, which thou knowest not"* (Jeremiah 33:3).

One night I was body surfing when I noticed something black flash around me. It happened so fast that I didn't have time to panic! It was there, and then it wasn't. That night there were three or four of us boys swimming together. I was catching a wave when I first saw the fin. It looked black and was riding a wave near me. This was very peculiar, because the sharks we would find already dead, or see around the piers were always blue or gray—not black.

I thought for a shark the surf was something to avoid, and this image of "being at odds" always made me feel a little more secure. Soon more waves were breaking, and I was on my way towards shore. Then I saw it again—and this time, I could see that the creature was only a curious seal wanting to play. Thank You, Lord.

Several years later, I was swimming with high school friends near a California beach and power station. The ocean water followed a channel that led to the power station. The water would enter the station cold, but it would come out warm. After swimming in the cool ocean, the warm water felt wonderful.

I remember two channels: one flowing into the plant, and the other flowing out. Using the channel, we would swim less than 100 feet and reach an inner plant vault. A concrete wall divided the warm and cold water, but at the end of the wall they converged, causing whirlpools to form where the channels began.

Although we sensed danger, we failed to truly understand the seriousness of our situation. We took turns swimming around the end of the inner wall, trying to avoid the whirlpools, and then letting the force of the warm water carry us back toward the ocean. Looking back, I realize we were all risking our lives in the name of fun, sport, and play. We were ignoring the immediate reality of drowning and the remote danger of encountering a shark.

I was in my twenties when I changed my mind about the danger of encountering a shark. After a day of sailing, I realized just how fortunate I was. As I sailed around the jetty into the marina, I couldn't help but notice a crowd of people gathering around the fishing-boat landing. From my boat, I could see what had to be a large shark.

After I had parked my boat and the trailer, I went straight to the landing. From there, I could see an Australian white shark hanging from the hoist. The shark was longer than the hoist was high. This was surprising, and later I found out that it had been killed off shore at the same stretch of beach where I had been day sailing.

The shark was seventeen feet long, weighed approximately 2,500 pounds, and had three rows of razor-sharp teeth. Next to my sloop, the shark was two feet longer on both ends. It was a monster, wide enough and long enough to swallow a person in one gulp.

I pray that kids today are less foolish and have better things to do than swim at night or near a power station. I believe that I am here today because I had a mother and grandmother praying for me. God is merciful, and He alone is worthy of our praise.

> *Ye have not chosen me, but I have chosen you, and ordained you, that ye should go and bring forth fruit, and that your fruit should remain: that whatsoever ye shall ask of the Father in my name, he may give it you* (John 15:16).

Driving North

I lived with my grandmother the summer before my senior year of high school. My parents had moved to central California, and I was staying behind to graduate.

Although I loved being with my grandmother, I was ready to visit my parents after only a few weeks of separation from them. I had driven city and coutnry roads and had taken some short road trips, but those trips had not prepared me for the two-lane roads crisscrossing central California.

I diligently studied a map and found the most direct route between my grandmother's home and where my parents were living. I was certain I could make the trip in one day. I would drive the Maricopa Highway towards Taft, crossing over the Los Padres

Mountains, and then head straight north up the Central Valley Region. I was overconfident, but I felt that I would be in good hands.

I was doing fine until I was about fifty miles south of where my parents lived. That is when I made an error in judgement and crashed my car. The road was a long two-lane stretch that went up over a hill, and until I was over that hill, I could not see how the road curved sharply to the left. Being young, and thinking I was invincible, I tried to negotiate the curve without slowing to a safe speed. As a result, I rolled the car over a couple of times.

What I remembered afterwards was the final roll, when the car landed on its wheels. I was not hurt, but the car was in a farmer's field with the front end pointed straight toward the road. After bending the cooling fan blades back away from the radiator, I was able to start the car. Because of the soft ground, however, the tires had no traction. You can probably guess what was going through my mind: I thought if I started the car, put it in drive, and got behind it to push, I could reach the road. My idea worked—until the car hit solid ground, and then it drove off without me! I am thankful that when my driverless car crossed the road, there were no other cars on the road.

Then I had a new dilemma: I was stuck on the other side of the road, only this time, the front of the car was facing *away* from the road. From the field I could not see much—maybe a few oil derricks. I knew I was in my grandmother's prayers when the farmer showed up. He decided that since I had already been in two fields in the same accident, the best thing to do was to use his tractor to pull me out. It was easy work for the farmer; in only minutes, I was thanking him and driving north again. God is merciful.

I am not sure if my parents were more surprised to see me, or to see the condition of my car; either way, they were glad to see me, and glad that I was not hurt. We had a good visit, but after a few days, I was ready to get back home. I had no problems whatsoever on my return trip.

The car, however, was never the same after that. It took a year, with a friend's help, to pound out the dents. I wanted to put the accident behind me, so I sold my wreck of a car soon after my friend's father painted it.

God uses all things for good. My parents never said, and I never asked the reason, but they moved back to southern California before my fall semester started.

> *And it shall come to pass, that before they call, I will answer; and while they are yet speaking, I will hear* (Isaiah 65:24).

We Called Her Gram

My natural mother lived with a heart condition—the result of having had rheumatic fever—until she died at the age of thirty-six. I was only eight years old, and all I thought about was my hurt and her pain—I blamed God for both. Although I was angry with God for what had happened, He was still watching over me. My grandmother, whom we affectionately called "Gram," came to live with us and take care of me. *"I will not leave you comfortless: I will come to you"* (John 14:18).

He blessed me with a God-loving and God-fearing grandmother, and I experienced the power of Christ's love through her love for me. She introduced me to Jesus, gave me my first Bible, and took me to church.

> *Be strong and of a good courage, fear not, nor be afraid of them: for the LORD thy God, he it is that doth go with thee; he will not fail thee, nor forsake thee* (Deuteronomy 31:6).

I have some loving memories of Gram, which include going swimming and taking a trip to Manson, Iowa. I remember that we were driving down the road, listening to music, when I began thumping the car roof with my hand. In the back seat, it sounded like I was keeping time with the music; but after Gram pulled over, I found out that from the front seat, it sounded like a flat tire. She turned the radio off and we resumed our trip. I was quiet after that.

God promises never to leave us or forsake us. I believe He puts people in each other's lives to minister

His love and promises. I remember hearing Gram recite the Lord's Prayer, read the Psalms, and pray for all her grandchildren and great-grandchildren.

My grandmother lived to be ninety-three. I'll always love her. In our family, she was the one who would say, "God love you," or "Bless your heart."

After my grandmother passed away, the one thing I wanted most to remember her by was her Bible—and thanks to my sister Joann Marie, I was the beneficiary. Our grandmother's Bible reads, "The Holy Bible presented to Bertha M. Egli by Ruth, Helen, and Verl. Christmas of 81." This keepsake is a blessing, because with it, we know exactly which verses she read, highlighted in yellow, and memorized. We know because of bent index-tabs, ear-marked pages, book markers, notes, and handwritten prayers.

For years, I wondered how my grandmother could keep her faith and trust in God after losing her only child. Today, however, I realize that she knew in her heart that it was a blessing, for it brought an end to my mother's pain and suffering. The Bible tells us: *"But my God shall supply all your need according to his riches in glory by Christ Jesus"* (Philippians 4:19).

Looking Beyond Yourself

Linda and I were married for two years before we each accepted Jesus Christ as our personal Lord and Savior.

Before we had an opportunity to find any outside support, however, we moved to the Pacific Northwest.

Once we were in Washington, we met a Silverdale realtor who helped us to find a home and a church, and to get acquainted with other members of the church who were in our age group. We will forever be in his debt. One of Blaine's first questions to us was, "Do you have a church?" And with that, he made sure we were securely established in a house of the Lord before he moved on.

Over the years, Linda became increasingly more devoted to God, while my focus was on building a house, going to college, and investing as a way of saving. These things were important, but they did not serve me spiritually. Spiritually speaking, I was a casualty of war. My spiritual life was at a standstill, God stayed real to me, but my old nature was still in control.

Only recently have I started looking for spiritual answers beyond Linda, beyond her daily prayer, devotion, worship, and love for God, or any realm of church or state. Although Linda has changed my life, I am realizing that it is not about you or me, and it is not about a spouse or a church—it is about God. God is here for us, and all we have to do is acknowledge Him.

When we pray and abide in His will, He is faithful to those of us who believe. *"Draw nigh to God, and he will draw nigh to you"* (James 4:8). He wants us to accept

His promises and to be our Lord and Savior: *"Humble yourselves in the sight of the Lord, and he shall lift you up"* (James 4:10).

When we look for Him and submit ourselves to Him with a heart for Jesus, God promises to lift us up and draw us near. My faith is in Him, whom I trust, believe, and obey.

> *He that hath my commandments, and keepeth them, he it is that loveth me: and he that loveth me shall be loved of my Father, and I will love him, and will manifest myself to him* (John 14:21).

Promises From God's Word

God's promises are blessings of grace, love, and mercy through which He reveals His truth and righteousness. This chapter features a few of God's promises to illustrate their importance, to show how much He blesses us, and to give each reader an opportunity to acknowledge how she or he is blessed.

> *For the mountains shall depart, and the hills be removed; but my kindness shall not depart from thee, neither shall the covenant of my peace be removed, saith the Lord that hath mercy on thee* (Isaiah 54:10).

CHAPTER SEVEN

Promises From God's Word

To Never Leave Us or Forsake Us

The Bible teaches us about the Father, the Son, and the Holy Spirit. When we accept Jesus as our Lord and Savior, we become filled with the Holy Spirit, God's seal of salvation.

God is our Father, Savior, Creator, Redeemer, Healer, and Lord. He wants us to know Him, to both fear and respect His power, authority, and judgement, and at the same time be encouraged and blessed by His grace, mercy, and loving kindness.

God planned our salvation only through the person of His Son, Jesus Christ. He sent Jesus to die on the cross for the sins of all mankind that we might have everlasting life through His death and resurrection. The Bible reveals that he who believes in God the Father and Jesus the Son will be received into Heaven, and will dwell in the house of the Lord forever. Jesus said that He would go and prepare a place for us, send the Holy Spirit to comfort us, and will some day return to take us home.

Through the ages—from the very beginning of time—God's promises have endured. He continues to love us and provide for our needs; He uses His power for good, and He promises His retribution and vengeance against our enemies:

> *To me* belongeth *vengeance and recompence; their foot shall slide in* due *time: for the day of their calamity is at hand, and the things that shall come upon them make haste* (Deuteronomy 32:35).

God's inspired Word tells us that God is all-present, all-knowing, and all-powerful, and that His faithfulness and love will neither fail us nor be taken from us. Therefore, we can trust in God's righteousness and everlasting love through our Lord and Savior, Jesus Christ:

> *I give them eternal life, and they shall never perish; no one can snatch them out of my hand. My Father, who has given them to me, is greater than all; no one can snatch them out of my Father's hand* (John 10:28–29, NIV).

To Answer Our Prayers

God promises to answer our prayers. By His given Word, we can know with assurance that He hears and answers our prayers. In our prayers, He hears our praise and worship. Whenever we give God credit and acknowledge Him, we are giving Him our praise and our worship. *"Great is the LORD, and greatly to be praised in the city of our God, in the mountain of his holiness"* (Psalm 48:1).

By living our lives for Christ, our prayers are not hindered, but rather answered. He wants us to call Him *Abba* (Aramaic for our word "Dad"); to cast our fears before Him; to give Him thanks, and to rejoice in Him.

God already knows what is within us—our cries, our pleas, and our requests. He understands our every need before we even ask. We minister one to another as He directs our paths.

I would like to share one answered prayer from Linda's daily journal:

"Lord, I pray that You would give me a tender heart toward all people. help me to see people as You see them. Help me to see their needs and respond as You would respond...Amen." (LMW: dated 05/19/2003)

Be careful for nothing; but in every thing by prayer and supplication with thanksgiving let your requests be made known unto God. And the peace of God, which passeth all understanding, shall keep your hearts and minds through Christ Jesus (Philippians 4:6–7).

To Make All Things Work Together for Good

In this world, bad things occur for a myriad of reasons—sometimes they happen naturally, and sometimes they are a result of our choices. Regardless of who or what is to blame, God will use both good and bad things for the good of those who love Him.

He *is* merciful. Although He may use the results of our bad choices for good, and forgive us our sins, He does not spare us from the consequences of our sinful actions. The consequences of sin will still fall upon the offender.

> *And we know that all things work together for good to them that love God, to them who are the called according to his purpose* (Romans 8:28).

Through the blessings God bestows on us, we are able to share *our* blessings with others, and also to be blessed in the process. Therefore, when we share God's blessings through our love for Him, we are privileged to be part of His plan to make all things work together for good.

God tells us how we can love him. He said,

> *He that hath my commandments, and keepeth them, he it is that loveth me: and he that loveth me shall be loved of my Father, and I will love him, and will manifest myself to him* (John 14:21).

He wants our love, devotion, and prayers, and He wants us to love one another through Him.

When we pray for others, we are petitioning God on their behalf. I believe prayer is one of those "things" that God uses to work together for good. When you love the Lord, He may use one person's prayer to meet another's need. In Colossians, we are told, *"Continue in prayer, and watch in the same with thanksgiving"* (Colossians 4:2).

God uses the power of our prayers to encourage us for "good." He said, *"Call unto me, and I will answer thee, and show thee great and mighty things, which thou knowest not"* (Jeremiah 33:3).

We may not understand or comprehend how God works all things together for good; but if we submit our lives to Him and seek His inspired Word, He will teach us about His Kingdom, His power, and how He is glorified through us by the power of the Holy Spirit. The Lord's Prayer tells us: *"...For thine is the kingdom, and the power, and the glory, for ever. Amen"* (Matthew 6:13).

To Sustain Us

Recently, a friend shared with me that "God will not give us more than we can handle":

> *There hath no temptation taken you but such as is common to man: but God is faithful, who will not suffer you to be tempted above that ye are able; but will with the temptation also make a way to escape, that ye may be able to bear it* (1 Corinthians 10:13).

I thought my friend had shared a wonderful promise. It seemed right, and sounded familiar; yet, I wondered about the cruel, unfair, and unreasonable life experiences we all have. The answer may lie in the fact that we live in a world that is tainted with the results of sin—both original sin and our sins.

God created all things for His glory and purpose. In God, this life is just the beginning. We do not know His exact will for our lives, but according to His Word, we know He is faithful.

> *Therefore if any man be in Christ, he is a new creature: old things are passed away; behold, all things are become new* (2 Corinthians 5:17).

According to Philippians 4:13, "*I can do all things through Christ which strengtheneth me.*" God won't test us by giving us more than we can handle, but at the same time, we are not to test God: "*Ye shall not tempt the LORD your God...*" (Deuteronomy 6:16). Therefore, we can trust in God, put our faith in God, and still know this world is not perfect.

We need Christ; He is our Savior, our Lord, and our Intercessor with God.

> *Wherefore he is able also to save them to the uttermost that come unto God by him, seeing he ever liveth to make intercession for them* (Hebrews 7:25).

The Bible does tell us about *too much burden*. It says that God will sustain us, lift us up, and that He won't let us fall. I thank the Lord for His Holy Word; without it, there would be chaos and confusion. Each person would have his or her own doctrine. Fortunately, we do not have to assume, take what we read at face value, or believe everything we hear. The Scriptures tell us,

> *For the prophecy came not in old time by the will of man: but holy men of God spake as they were moved by the Holy Ghost* (2 Peter 1:21).

Although reading the Bible may not diminish life's challenges, it *does* tell us what to expect and how to respond. Life's challenges will always be with us. In Christ, whenever we make a bad choice, He will use our situation for good and, at the same time, show us his definition of obedience, trust, forgiveness, faithfulness and dependency.

God does not promise us an easy life. For example, a person who is on a recipient list for a transplant may have all he can handle within the confines of his own strength, but the person who believes in God he can cast his anxieties on Him and draw on the Lord's Strength. We can trust Him to prepare our way, to guide our paths, and to make ready a place for us.

Through the Scriptures, we are encouraged to lean on God—to lay our burdens at His feet, and let Him work through us and be our strength. Our Lord is a merciful and benevolent God, and He is glorified in our weakness—not in the fact that we are suffering. We can rely on His promises to love us, to comfort us, and to sustain us in our times of trouble, need and fear.

> *Cast thy burden upon the* LORD, *and he shall sustain thee: he shall never suffer the righteous to be moved* (Psalm 55:22).

Retribution Against Our Enemies Is His

When other people commit transgressions against us, God expects our trust and faithfulness by acknowledging Him. He wants us to keep our commitments before Christ, to turn the violations or crimes over to Him, and to forgive our perpetrators, as He forgives us.

As a Christian I believe in God, the Father, Son, and Holy Spirit, I believe in Jesus Chrst and the Holy Bible, that all creation is God's domain, and God has the authority over all things. I believe in God's salvation, that people are Spirit-filled, God's understanding is beyond ours, and only God is omnipresent, omniscient, and omnipotent; meaning He is all-present, all-knowing, and all-powerful.

I believe His Word gives us hope and teaches us how to develop faith, forgiveness, and trust, while His promises take into account love, mercy, and grace in lieu of retribution and judgement. Because I believe in God, His Word, promises, and blessings, I believe there will be days of judgment, punishment, and retribution, as well as days of triumph, jubilation, and joy.

In truth, when we live a life for Christ and someone commits a wrong against us, he or she is committing a wrong against Him. Because we are all His creations and will each be judged, He will eventually have the vengeance.

> *For we know him that hath said, Vengeance* belongeth *unto me, I will recompense, saith the Lord. And again, The Lord shall judge his people. It is a fearful thing to fall into the hands of the living God* (Hebrews 10:30–31).

Give and It Will Be Given

People enjoy giving. When you give, you have a chance to make someone else happy, and that makes you happy. It's a two-way street, and a perfect example of God's love.

Our God is a giving God who created man in His image and who wants us to live a life for Christ. He wants us to give from our hearts and from our abundance, to be generous and unselfish, to reach out to those in need, and to help those who are unable to help themselves.

Jesus tells us to:

Give, and it shall be given unto you; good measure, pressed down, and shaken together, and running over, shall men give into your bosom. For with the same measure that ye mete withal it shall be measured to you again (Luke 6:38).

When we have a heart for giving, God will give to us in return until our cups are running over. Therefore, we will never be able to outgive Him. The Bible teaches us that we are blessed when we give, so we do so out of our obedience to God.

Through our giving, someone is blessed; God is glorified, exalted, and blessed; and in return, *we* are blessed. Jesus said that *"It is more blessed to give than to receive"* (Acts 20:35).

Prayers

This chapter contains five prayers for the reader. The first is a prayer of surrender, and it asks the Lord to take away our old carnal nature. The second, a daily prayer, asks God to maintain His perfect will over our lives. The third is a hedge-of-protection prayer for all children, grandchildren, and great-grandchildren. The fourth is an all-inclusive, lifelong prayer. And the fifth is The Lord's Prayer.

> *Be careful for nothing; but in every thing by prayer and supplication with thanksgiving let your requests be made known unto God. And the peace of God, which passeth all understanding, shall keep your hearts and minds through Christ Jesus* (Philippians 4:6–7).

CHAPTER EIGHT

Prayers

A Surrender Prayer

God, please hear my prayer. I ask you to forgive my disobedience, anger, and contempt. I pray for the courage, strength and power that I need to conquer my old carnal nature.

My desire is to live for Jesus, to keep my Father's commandments, to abide in His love, to seek God first in all things and to serve Him only. I wish to relinquish control of my life to God, die to self, surrender my pride and selfishness, and stop my demanding and self-serving ways.

I pray that I accept God's will and desire for my heart. In Jesus' name I pray, Amen.

Therefore if any man be in Christ, he is a new creature: old things are passed away; behold, all things are become new (2 Corinthians 5:17).

A Daily Prayer

Dear God, I thank You for this day, and I desire Your strength and power over it. I pray today is the day; a day of friendship, forgiveness, and compassion.

I ask that You use me, and that Your will be done in me and through me. I pray for those in need, for the sick and the hungry. Please have mercy on them, Father, giving each one their full measure of days, and a blessed victory over today.

I seek Your presence, Oh Living God, for in Your presence I will be changed.

Amen.

Fear thou not; for I am with thee: be not dismayed; for I am *thy God: I will strengthen thee; yea, I will help thee; yea, I will uphold thee with the right hand of my righteousness* (Isaiah 41:10).

A Hedge-of-Protection Prayer

Dear God, I thank You for children, grandchildren, and great-grandchildren: "*...for of such is the kingdom of heaven.*"[1] I pray that You will draw them close, and that they will seek Your salvation in the name of Jesus Christ.

I ask for a hedge of protection over them, and for their eyes to be opened, so they will see Your truth. I pray that each day, they will submit themselves to You and long to hear Your call.

As their Shepherd, please grant them Your love, mercy, and grace for the rest of their days.

Amen.

A Lifelong Prayer

Dear Lord, if I had but one prayer, I would pray to have but one promise.

If I had but one promise, I would promise God, country, myself, wife, family, relatives, friends, church, co-workers, neighbors, the elderly, the underprivileged, the disabled, the disadvantaged, and the handicapped to keep my word, be thankful, and to pray about each new day.

If I had but one promise, I would promise to share God's love and to be encouraged, obedient, and faithful. To smile and be accepting of others. To help feed the hungry and remember what's important. To be honest, trustworthy, and my own best friend. To forgive myself and others, appreciate diversity, and be open-minded.

If I had but one promise, I would promise to pull my own weight, visit the sick, maintain a teachable spirit, and keep things in perspective. To be in the present. To be generous and brave and to obey God's commandments. To be organized, to save for a rainy day, mind my own business, keep a sense of humor, and to write things down.

If I had but one promise, I would promise to live the life God gave me, give of myself, be willing to listen to others, stay in touch with loved ones, and take care of my health and spiritual life. To stay the course, run the distance, fight a good fight, and be a caring citizen of the world.

Thank you, Jesus. Amen.

The Lord's Prayer

Our Father which art in heaven,
Hallowed be thy name.
Thy kingdom come,
Thy will be done in earth,
as it is in heaven.
Give us this day our daily bread.
And forgive us our debts,
as we forgive our debtors.
And lead us not into temptation,
but deliver us from evil:
For thine is the kingdom,
and the power, and the glory,
for ever. Amen
(Matthew 6:9–13).

Notes

[1] *"But Jesus said, Suffer little children, and forbid them not, to come unto me: for of such is the kingdom of heaven'"* (Matthew 19:14).

Prose and Poetry

Most of the prose and poems appearing in this chapter reiterate the subject and theme of this book. Hopefully, they will add additional meaning, power, and purpose to a promise.

I believe promises are essential because they serve God. They reflect our spiritual health, strengthen and build our relationships, and provide a perfect means by which to express God's love.

Great is the LORD, and greatly to be praised in the city of our God, in the mountain of his holiness (Psalm 48:1).

CHAPTER NINE

Prose and Poetry

1. "From Love and Duty"

From love and duty come special PROMISES,
yours for the making.
From PROMISES kept come respect and honor,
yours for the keeping.

2. "Giving Focus"

PROMISES provide important direction and meaning,
in a private and personal way.
Where sincere acts of compassion
with purpose of heart,
give focus so not to stray.

3. "Grace Is His Proof"

I once thought seeing better forward after
looking backward was part of
God's PROMISES; instead it was a

remnant of my youth.
When I was growing up, experience was my teacher.
I had more faith in
God-given talent, than I did in Jesus and His truth.
But God's righteousness will not be denied.
In the name of Jesus Christ,
He is loving and merciful, and grace is His proof.

4. "A Promise Is Realized"

As your PROMISES are realized, more worthy you'll be
with whom you have PROMISED and
those you disagree.

5. "In the Heart"

In his heart, she is on sacred ground.
In her heart, he is homeward bound.
In her love, God's PROMISES abound.
In his love, God's PROMISES are found.

6. "Whatever It Was"

I wanted whatever the old man had
without first knowing
what it was, or how to get it.
There was nothing in his facial expression,
that suggested anything but merit.
Only a PROMISE to God to die to self
and live for Christ,
sealed by the presence of the Holy Spirit.

7. "Making a Promise"

Make a PROMISE, make a friend.
Keep a PROMISE, keep a friend.

8. "Self-Respect"

When we keep our PROMISES,
we keep our self-respect.
To whom we have given our word,
they know what to expect.

9. "Opened Doors"

Be encouraged by PROMISES of opened doors,
until your closed doors are repealed.
Be blessed by PROMISES of closed doors,
while your opened doors are revealed.

10. "Fruit of the Spirit"

A wonderful provision worth understanding
may be difficult, but not too steep.
Something special that happens within us
for the PROMISES we keep.
Surpassing any contribution or achievement
manifested without a peep.
It is the fruit of the Spirit, which He gives,
that comforts us to sleep.

11. "A Moral Truism"

A PROMISE is a PROMISE is a moral truism,
relying on its unique and perfect essence.
Thus PROMISES are perceived as equivalent,
whether their size is minute or immense.
Only pure logic equates keeping a PROMISE
on par with establishing sound precedence.

12. "The Old Carnal Man"

According to the old carnal man in me, my PROMISE
to surrender made him the victim.
My carnal man had no intention or desire to leave,
so my decision was to evict him.

13. "A Ball of Colored Twine"

PROMISES kept are memories we keep,
as treasures to glimmer and shine.
Treasured memories are linked one to another,
as the colors in a ball of colored twine.
What triggers our memory may help to unravel
the memories of an earlier paradigm.

14. "A Loyal Act of Courage"

PROMISES can span many generations,
creating tangible ways to encourage.
To preserve a second-hand PROMISE,
is itself a loyal act of courage.

15. "Life's Promises"

Life demands to share its PROMISES,
they are passed from age to age.
From life's PROMISES come life's lessons,
a person's living legacy to old age.

16. "Sharing God's Love"

When a person shares love and commitment
together with his PROMISES,
he shows faithfulness.
Out of faithfulness a PROMISE is realized
yielding God's blessed love,
to experience and witness.
The fruit of the Spirit that is revealed,
when nourished and preserved,
exemplifies God's goodness.

17. "The Christian Soldier"

I see a PROMISE between man and Maker;
'tis after the old man surrenders as the beholder,
that God considers him to be a Christian soldier.

18. "A Generous Gift"

PROMISES may overcome a rash of sorrow and greed,
obliterating reasons for a fray.
But for such a generous gift of love and kindness,
our life goes on display.

19. "God's Promenade"

It is through the power of the love of Christ,
that the PROMISE of marriage
is made perfect unto God.
God can take a PROMISE that is half facade,
and use it to help us perceive
His heavenly promenade.

20. "Without Him"

It's possible to have a life without Him.
You can PROMISE to reach the tallest limb.
Or bet your entire life on a whim.
But you don't want to die without Him.

21. "Second Chance"

I wish I had a second chance;
I would give it a different spin.
To know then what I know now
I'd live my life over again.
I would seek the Lord and die to self
surrender, and not abstain.
On my honor, I'd keep my PROMISES
using my left-most brain.

22. "God Is Real"

When I consider life's PROMISES,
it is clear my need for God is real.
When I examine that which really counts,
I thank God for the privilege to kneel.
When I think about my salvation,
it is Christ's love that I feel.

23. "Looking Forward to Meeting You"

I know heaven is a challenge for the well-to-do,
while mine is what I thought I knew.
Because it's a life of Christ I pursue, a prayer
and a PROMISE, changed my venue.
Dear God, I'm thankful to be born anew, and to be
looking forward to meeting You.

24. "For My Mother"

My grandmother would say,
"Honey it's okay, he knows the way."
"I know, dear," my mother would say,
"He was my PROMISE to God today."

25. "It Is God's Love"

If someone is better off because of a PROMISE,
then keeping it is God's blessing.
Therefore when we are obedient and faithful,
it is God's love we are expressing.

26. "God's Foundation"

When making a PROMISE,
do you consider it to be new?
Or from a humble beginning,
is it God's will for you?
Does the PROMISE seem selfish
until you follow through?
By building on God's foundation,
our PROMISES are made true.

27. "Chicken Soup"

You wanted chicken soup to warm your soul,
He has living water to fill your bowl.
Keeping your PROMISE was your goal,
by His grace He makes you whole.

28. "Jesus Was God's Promise"

What gives a PROMISE, PROMISE?
Is it all the tangibles and intangibles,
the obedience to God,
the dying to self,
or is it the life of Christ,
that gives a PROMISE, PROMISE?

29. "The Second Life"

If I had a second life to live,
the first would be reversed.

Confidently I would pray to Christ,
the PROMISE I'd rehearsed.
That each and every day in Him,
would be just like the first.

30. "Fare-Thee-Well"

If the reason for a PROMISE is unworthy,
the PROMISE will be as well.
Either find a PROMISE that is worth keeping
or bid it, "Fare-thee-well."

31. "The Bottom Line"

The quote, "You do your part, and I'll do mine"
is a PROMISE that seems right, and sounds fine,
but it is not in the Bible, which is a doubtful sign.
God said, "You are the branches, I am the Vine."[1]
Let your relationship with Him be your bottom line,
and flow from whatever you do in the face of time.

32. "Jesus Is Our Right of Passage"

The expression, "God helps those who help themselves,"
is a faulty adage rather than a Holy Bible passage.
The Bible tells us, "God helps those who *cannot* help
themselves;"[2] only in Him there is no bondage.
I claim in the name of Christ, God's PROMISES,
His perfect will, and Jesus as my right of passage.

33. "A True Chord"

When a person sees "something" that strikes
a true chord. Pray that the "something" is what God
will afford, and be thankful for God's PROMISES
unto the glory of the Lord.

34. "The Saving Knowledge of You"

I pray that children are less foolish than we were,
and that they have better things to do.
Lord, I ask that You bless and keep them,
to help make their PROMISES come true.
I pray for their health and well being,
and for their saving knowledge of You.
Please Lord, give them Your love, mercy, and
grace,and a deserving point of view.

35. "Making Moral Changes"

PROMISES express intentions of good,
"from now on I'll do better."
The things we do from day-to-day,
"from here on will matter."

36. "Grace Period"

I gave my old nature a twenty-year grace period,
to relinquish power and control.
It was self-serving and focused,
while I PROMISED that God had my soul.
Now I abide in Jesus Christ, my Lord and Savior,
with God's will my ultimate goal.

37. "In Due Course"

I thank God for His Holy Word,
for without it there would be
complete chaos, confusion, and no remorse.
God does not PROMISE a perfect life,
only Jesus had that distinction.
But, He does PROMISE eternal life, in due course.

38. "My Best Promises"

I have made PROMISES I did not keep,
some were even contrived.
When I look at life's PROMISES,
I'm grateful Lord, I survived.
My best PROMISES are those I keep,
where no one is deprived.
Someday I'll say, "By the Grace of God,
I, too, have arrived!"

39. "Word for Word"

When we seek God's greatest PROMISE,
it is Jesus Christ who has no rival.
If it seems right and it sounds familiar,
but it is not PROMISED in the Bible,
Ask, "Does it embrace His righteous past,
sacrificial love, and future arrival?"

40. "Among our Greatest Possessions"

By His stripes we are healed;
blessed beyond compare.
By His love we are blessed,
covered by answered prayer.
To believe PROMISES are worth keeping,
is believing He is why we care.

Notes

[1] *"I am the vine, ye are the branches: He that abideth in me, and I in him, the same bringeth forth much fruit: for without me ye can do nothing"* (John 15:5).

[2] *"For he shall deliver the needy when he crieth; the poor also, and him that hath no helper. He shall spare the poor and needy, and shall save the souls of the needy"* (Psalm 72:12–13).

Bible Verses

This list of Bible verses includes passages quoted throughout this book; some have appeared more than once. There are also some verses listed solely for the sake of organization, relevance, or because of their relative importance.

But my God shall supply all your need according to his riches in glory by Christ Jesus (Philippians 4:19).

CHAPTER TEN

Bible Verses

Introduction

1. "And ye shall know the truth, and the truth shall make you free" (John 8:32).

2. "Give, and it shall be given unto you; good measure, pressed down, and shaken together, and running over, shall men give into your bosom. For with the same measure that ye mete withal it shall be measured to you again" (Luke 6:38).

Chapter 1

3. "How excellent is thy lovingkindness, O God! therefore the children of men put their trust under the shadow of thy wings" (Psalm 36:7).

4. "Being confident of this very thing, that he which hath begun a good work in you will perform it until the day of Jesus Christ" (Philippians 1:6).

5. "Call unto me, and I will answer thee, and show thee great and mighty things, which thou knowest not" (Jeremiah 33:3).

6. "And it shall come to pass afterward, that I will pour out my spirit upon all flesh; and your sons and your daughters shall prophesy, your old men shall dream dreams, your young men shall see visions" (Joel 2:28).

Chapter 2

7. "The fear of the LORD *is* the beginning of knowledge: but fools despise wisdom and instruction" (Proverbs 1:7).

8. "In Gibeon the LORD appeared to Solomon in a dream by night: and God said, Ask what I shall give thee" (1 Kings 3:5).

9. "Jesus saith unto him, 'I am the way, the truth, and the life: no man cometh unto the father, but by me'" (John 14:6).

10. "'Behold, I stand at the door, and knock: if any man hear my voice, and open the door, I will come in to him, and will sup with him, and he with me'" (Revelation 3:20).

11. "Behold, I have done according to thy words: lo, I have given thee a wise and an understanding heart; so that there was none like thee before

thee, neither after thee shall any arise like unto thee" (1 Kings 3:12).

12. "God gave Solomon wisdom and very great insight, and a breadth of understanding as measureless as the sand on the seashore. Solomon's wisdom was greater than the wisdom of all the men of the East, and greater than all the wisdom of Egypt. He was wiser than any other man, including Ethan the Ezrahite—wiser than Heman, Calcol and Darda, the sons of Mahol. And his fame spread to all the surrounding nations." (1 Kings 4:29–31, NIV).

13. "For the Lord giveth wisdom: out of his mouth cometh knowledge and understanding" (Proverbs 2:6).

14. "Counsel is mine, and sound wisdom: I am understanding; I have strength" (Proverbs 8:14).

15. "Therefore if any man be in Christ, he is a new creature: old things are passed away; behold, all things are become new" (2 Corinthians 5:17).

16. "For he shall deliver the needy when he crieth; the poor also, and him that hath no helper. He shall spare the poor and needy, and shall save the souls of the needy" (Psalm 72:12–13).

Chapter 3

** (Luke 6:38) Defined in the introduction.

17. "I have shewed you all things, how that so labouring ye ought to support the weak, and to remember the words of the Lord Jesus, how he said, 'It is more blessed to give than to receive'" (Acts 20:35).

18. "Every man according as he purposeth in his heart, so let him give: not grudgingly, or of necessity: for God loveth a cheerful giver " (2 Corinthians 9:7).

** (Proverbs 1:7) Defined in chapter 2.

Chapter 4

19. "For ye are all the children of God by faith in Christ Jesus" (Galatians 3:26).

Chapter 5

20. "But my God shall supply all your need according to his riches in glory by Christ Jesus" (Philippians 4:19).

21. "'For God so loved the world, that he gave his only begotten Son, that whosoever believeth in him should not perish, but have everlasting life'" (John 3:16).

22. "'I am the vine, ye are the branches: He that abideth in me, and I in him, the same bringeth forth much fruit: for without me ye can do nothing'" (John 15:5).

23. "'No man can serve two masters: for either he will hate the one, and love the other; or else he will hold to the one, and despise the other. Ye cannot serve God and mammon'" (Matthew 6:24).

24. "'Ye have not chosen me, but I have chosen you, and ordained you, that ye should go and bring forth fruit, and that your fruit should remain: that whatsoever ye shall ask of the Father in my name, he may give it you'" (John 15:16).

** (Galatians 3:26) Defined in chapter 4.

** (2 Corinthians 5:17) Defined in chapter 2.

25. "In whom ye also trusted, after that ye heard the word of truth, the gospel of your salvation: in whom also after that ye believed, ye were sealed with that holy Spirit of promise," (Ephesians 1:13).

26. "Whoso findeth a wife findeth a good thing, and obtaineth favour of the LORD (Proverbs 18:22).

27. "Now therefore arise, O LORD God, into thy resting place, thou, and the ark of thy strength: let thy priests, O LORD God, be clothed with salvation, and let thy saints rejoice in goodness" (2 Chronicles 6:41).

Chapter 6

28. "And he said unto me, 'My grace is sufficient for thee: for my strength is made perfect in weakness.' Most gladly therefore will I rather glory in my infirmities, that the power of Christ may rest upon me" (2 Corinthians 12:9).

** (Jeremiah 33:3) Defined in chapter 1.

29. "'I will not leave you comfortless: I will come to you'" (John 14:18).

30. "Be strong and of a good courage, fear not, nor be afraid of them: for the LORD thy God, he it is that doth go with thee; he will not fail thee, nor forsake thee" (Deuteronomy 31:6).

31. "Draw nigh to God, and he will draw nigh to you. Cleanse your hands, ye sinners; and purify your hearts, ye double minded" (James 4:8).

32. "Humble yourselves in the sight of the Lord, and he shall lift you up" (James 4:10).

33. "'He that hath my commandments, and keepeth them, he it is that loveth me: and he that loveth me shall be loved of my Father, and I will love him, and will manifest myself to him'" (John 14:21).

34. "And it shall come to pass, that before they call, I will answer; and while they are yet speaking, I will hear" (Isaiah 65:24).

** (Philippians 4:19) Defined in chapter 5.

** (John 15:16) Defined in chapter 5.

Chapter 7

35. "For the mountains shall depart, and the hills be removed; but my kindness shall not depart from

thee, neither shall the covenant of my peace be removed, saith the LORD that hath mercy on thee" (Isaiah 54:10).

36. "Great is the Lord, and greatly to be praised in the city of our God, in the mountain of his holiness" (Psalm 48:1).

37. "For we know him that hath said, 'Vengeance belongeth unto me, I will recompense,' saith the Lord. And again, 'The Lord shall judge his people.' It is a fearful thing to fall into the hands of the living God" (Hebrews 10:30–31).

38. "To me belongeth vengeance, and recompence; their foot shall slide in due time: for the day of their calamity is at hand, and the things that shall come upon them make haste" (Deuteronomy 32:35).

39. "'I give them eternal life, and they shall never perish; no one can snatch them out of my hand. My Father, who has given them to me, is greater than all; no one can snatch them out of my Father's hand'" (John 10:28–29, NIV).

40. "Cast thy burden upon the LORD, and he shall sustain thee: he shall never suffer the righteous to be moved" (Psalm 55:22).

41. "Be careful for nothing; but in every thing by prayer and supplication with thanksgiving let your

requests be made known unto God. And the peace of God, which passeth all understanding, shall keep your hearts and minds through Christ Jesus" (Philippians 4:6–7).

42. "'And lead us not into temptation, but deliver us from evil: For thine is the kingdom, and the power, and the glory, for ever. Amen'" (Matthew 6:13).

43. "For the prophecy came not in old time by the will of man: but holy men of God spake as they were moved by the Holy Ghost" (2 Peter 1:21).

44. "Wherefore he is able also to save them to the uttermost that come unto God by him, seeing he ever liveth to make intercession for them" (Hebrews 7:25).

** (Luke 6:38) Defined in chapter 3.

45. "And we know that all things work together for good to them that love God, to them who are the called according to his purpose" (Romans 8:28).

** (John 14:21) Defined in chapter 6.

** (Jeremiah 33:3) Defined in chapters 1 and 6.

46. "There hath no temptation taken you but such as is common to man: but God is faithful, who will not suffer you to be tempted above that ye are able; but will with the temptation also make a way to escape, that ye may be able to bear it" (I Corinthians 10:13).

** (Acts 20:35) Defined in chapter 3.

47. "I can do all things through Christ which strength-eneth me" (Philippians 4:13).

** (2 Corinthians 5:17) Defined in chapters 2 and 5.

48. "Ye shall not tempt the Lord your God, as ye tempted him in Massah" (Deuteronomy 6:16).

Chapter 8

** (Philippians 4:6–7) Defined in chapter 7.

** (2 Corinthians 5:17) Defined in chapters 2, 5, and 7.

49."But Jesus said, 'Suffer little children, and forbid them not, to come unto me: for of such is the kingdom of heaven'" (Matthew 19:14).

** (Matthew 6:13) defined in chapter 7.

50. "Fear thou not; for I am with thee: be not dismayed; for I am thy God: I will strengthen thee; yea, I will help thee; yea, I will uphold thee with the right hand of my righteousness" (Isaiah 41:10).

Chapter 9

** (Psalm 72:12–13) Defined in chapter 2.

** (John 15:5) Defined in chapter 5.

** (Psalm 48:1) Defined in chapter 7.

Chapter 10

** (Philippians 4:19) Defined in chapters 5 and 6.

Supplementary Bible Verses:

** "'For where two or three are gathered together in my name, there am I in the midst of them'" (Matthew 18:20).

** "Thy word is a lamp unto my feet, and a light unto my path" (Psalm 119:105).

** "He is the Rock, his work is perfect: for all his ways are judgment: a God of truth and without iniquity, just and right is he" (Deuteronomy 32:4).

** "'If ye abide in me, and my words abide in you, ye shall ask what ye will, and it shall be done unto you'" (John 15:7).

** "'Blessed are they which do hunger and thirst after righteousness: for they shall be filled'" (Matthew 5:6).

** "'As the Father hath loved me, so have I loved you: continue ye in my love. If ye keep my commandments, ye shall abide in my love; even as I have kept my Father's commandments, and abide in his love'" (John 15:9–10).

** "'For what is a man profited, if he shall gain the whole world, and lose his own soul? or what shall a man give in exchange for his soul?'" (Matthew 16:26).

** "'Yea, though I walk through the valley of the shadow of death, I will fear no evil: for thou art with me; thy rod and thy staff they comfort me. Thou preparest a table before me in the presence of mine enemies: thou anointest my head with oil; my cup runneth over. Surely goodness and mercy shall follow me all the days of my life: and I will dwell in the house of the Lord for ever" (Psalm 23:4–6).

Chapter 11

51. "'But seek ye first the kingdom of God, and his righteousness; and all these things shall be added unto you'" (Matthew 6:33).

52. "'Not every one that saith unto me, 'Lord, Lord,' shall enter into the kingdom of heaven; but he that doeth the will of my Father which is in heaven. Many will say to me in that day, 'Lord, Lord, have we not prophesied in thy name? and in thy name have cast out devils? and in thy name done many wonderful works?' And then will I profess unto them, 'I never knew you: depart from me, ye that work iniquity'" (Matthew 7:21–23).

** (Matthew 6:13) Defined in chapters 7, and 8.

Conclusion

By looking at the old man, I could see the promise he was making to God. I felt humbled and privileged at the same time. My desire was to die to self, relinquish control, and seek the presence of our living God: "Please Lord, give me courage, strength, and power over thy enemy. In Jesus' name I pray, Amen."

It took answered prayer before I surrendered, but now I know Jesus as my Lord and Savior. It takes a commitment to live a life for Christ, so when our eyes are opened to God, the time is right to follow Him and to make our commitment of faith. *"But seek ye first the kingdom of God, and his righteousness..."* (Matthew 6:33).

His desire is for a lifelong relationship with us—one that deserves our commitment. Without a commitment, our relationship with Him is strained. Trying to serve God without having a relationship is even worse.

When we live outside of Christ, and at the same time claim to serve Him, it is displeasing to God:

Not every one that saith unto me, Lord, Lord, shall enter into the kingdom of heaven; but he that doeth the will of my Father which is in heaven. Many will say to me in that day, Lord, Lord, have we not prophesied in thy name? and in thy name have cast out devils? and in thy name done many wonderful works? And then will I profess unto them, I never knew you: depart from me, ye that work iniquity (Matthew 7:21–23).

Living for eternity with the Lord and Savior, Jesus Christ, is a choice. Therefore, it is imperative that we make our committed relationship with Him echo our decision. Being obedient to God gives Him a chance to work in our lives to bring about His purpose. Through a committed relationship of obedience and faithfulness, God can overpower, overcome, and overtake our faults, fears, and failures. When we are weak, He is strong; when we are troubled, He is wise; and when we are critical, He is accepting.

His love is unconditional, everlasting, and greater than any other. "...*For thine is the kingdom, and the power, and the glory, for ever. Amen*" (Matthew 6:13). Our senior pastor said it best: "Whatever you do for the rest of your life, let it flow out of your relationship with Jesus Christ."

My desire is that this book will glorify Christ by allowing Him to draw us closer, and prove beneficial and encouraging for all its readers.

CONTACT ADDRESSES

By mail:

Jon R. Wood
P.O. Box 1963
Kingston, Washington
98346

Over the Internet:

www.jonnwood.com

jonnwood@highstream.net